Laura Horton

Laura Horton is Plymouth Laureate of Words, 2021-22, the first playwright and woman in the position. In 2020 Horton wrote and produced her first film, *A Summer of Birds,* Toast of the Fringe winner. Plays include: *Labyrinth Diet*, The Space, London 2021, ONCOMM winner; Triptych, Theatre Royal Plymouth, 2021; *Giddy Tuppy*, The Space, ONCOMM winner, 2020; *This I Believe,* Theatre Royal Plymouth, Exeter Phoenix, 2019. She is currently commissioned by Theatre Royal Plymouth. She was listed in The Stage 100 in 2021 for her project Theatre Stories CIC. *Breathless* was selected for the Pleasance and Theatre Royal Plymouth Regional Partnership.

@LauraCHorton

First published in the UK in 2022 by Aurora Metro Publications Ltd

67 Grove Avenue, Twickenham, TW1 4HX

www.aurorametro.com   info@aurorametro.com

T: @aurorametro FB/AuroraMetroBooks

Breathless© 2022 Laura Horton

Cover photo courtesy of Laura Horton

Cover designed by Aurora Metro Books.

With many thanks to: Alice Billington

ISBN: 978-1-912430-83-3 print

978-1-912430-84-0 ebook

Breathless

by

Laura Horton

AURORA METRO BOOKS

Dedicated to my mum, dad
and brother,
whose unconditional love has
taught me everything.

Theatre
Royal
Plymouth

Theatre Royal Plymouth is a registered charity providing art, education and community engagement throughout Plymouth and the wider region. We engage and inspire many communities through performing arts and we aim to touch the lives and interests of people from all backgrounds. We do this by creating and presenting a breadth of shows on a range of scales, with our extensive creative engagement programmes, by embracing the vitality of new talent and supporting emerging and established artists, and by collaborating with a range of partners to provide dynamic cultural leadership for the city of Plymouth.

Follow @TRPlymouth on Twitter

Like Theatre Royal Plymouth at facebook.com/ TheatreRoyalPlymouth

Follow @theatreroyalplymouth on Instagram

Theatre Royal Plymouth, Royal Parade, Plymouth, PL1 2TR+ 44 (0) 1752 267222

info@theatreroyal.com www.theatreroyal.com

Registered Charity: 284545

Produced in National Partnership with Pleasance & Theatre Royal Plymouth. The National Partnerships see the Pleasance work with important venues nationwide to identify, recognise and fund extraordinary work from across the UK to be presented at the Fringe.

BY LAURA HORTON
PLYMOUTH LAUREATE OF WORDS 2021-22

Laura Horton and Theatre Royal Plymouth in association with Pleasance.

CAST:
Sophie – Madeleine MacMahon

CREATIVE TEAM:
WRITER Laura Horton
DIRECTOR Stephanie Kempson
DRAMATURGY Isabel Dixon
COMPOSER Verity Standen

Theatre Royal Plymouth

PRODUCTION TEAM:
HEAD OF PRODUCTION Hugh Borthwick
COSTUME SUPERVISOR Delia Lancaster
HEAD OF TECHNICAL Matt Hoyle
DRUM & LAB MANAGER John Purkis
HEAD OF SOUND Dan Mitcham
DEPUTY HEAD OF SOUND & SOUND DESIGNER Holly Harbottle

LIGHTING TECHNICIAN Pete Harbottle

MARKETING OFFICER Ellie Woolman

MEDIA & COMMUNICATION MANAGER Savanna Myszka

DIGITAL CONTENT AND MEDIA PRODUCER Chris Baker

TALENT DEVELOPMENT PRODUCER Ben Lyon-Ross

LEADERSHIP TEAM:

CHIEF EXECUTIVE James Mackenzie-Blackman

DIRECTOR OF ENGAGEMENT AND LEARNING Mandy Precious

OPERATIONS DIRECTOR Helen Costello

DIRECTOR OF AUDIENCE AND COMMUNICATIONS Suzi McGoldrick

HEAD OF PROJECT DEVELOPMENT Seb Soper

HEAD OF WORKSHOP Brendan Cusack

HEAD OF MARKETING Phillipa Revest

HEAD OF CONTRACTING Laura Edwards

HEAD OF FINANCE RISK AND IT Lewis Eynon

THEATRE MANAGER Jennifer Hopkins

HEAD OF TICKETING AND SALES Annette Earl

HEAD OF HR Deborah Clinton

HEAD OF LEARNING Jane Pawson

HEAD OF ESTATES John Spreadridge

HEAD OF PRODUCTION Hugh Borthwick

HEAD OF TECHNICAL Matt Hoyle

Supported using public funding by
ARTS COUNCIL ENGLAND

BIOGRAPHIES

Director: Stephanie Kempson

Stephanie Kempson is Artistic Director of Sharp Teeth Theatre (Associate Company with the Wardrobe Theatre), as a director/dramaturg she has worked with Bristol Old Vic, Bath Theatre Royal, The Egg Theatre, Tobacco Factory Theatres, Taunton Brewhouse, Shakespeare's Birthplace Trust, Compass Presents, SS Great Britain, Scratchworks Theatre, Serena Flynn, PeCo Theatre, Documental Theatre.

Performer: Madeleine MacMahon

Madeleine is an actor and comedian from Gloucestershire. In 2021 she won The Max Turner Prize, was a BBC New Comedy Longlister and Funny Women Semi-Finalist. Television: Eastenders; Doctors (BBC); The Freedoms (Amazon Prime).Theatre includes: A Super Happy Story (About Feeling Super Sad) (Silent Uproar); 21 Pounds; Cider With Rosie; (Cheltenham Everyman); Mercury Fur (Middle Child); Kings (New Diorama) and numerous panto's at Hereford Courtyard.

@madi_macmahon

Composer: Verity Standen

Verity Standen is a composer, director, performer and choir leader. Verity Standen's compositions include Hug (National & International tours), Mmm Hmmm (National tour), Symphony (National tour), Refrain (Situations), Undersong (Mayfest), Polyphony (Mayfest), Voices of Worle (Terrestrial), Where Do You Hide? (Mayk), Airborne (Royal Brompton & Harefield Hospitals Charity and rb&hArts).

CONTENTS

ABOUT THE PLAY

In 2021 I was approached by Theatre Royal Plymouth to research, develop and present a triptych of 20-minute plays. As time was short for my third piece I ended up penning a very personal piece about a woman moving back to Devon and struggling to navigate dating as a hoarder. *Suffocating Stuff* was born, performed by Zahra Ahmadi and directed by Phoebe Rhodes and the reaction to it was really powerful. I had many people approach me to say they thought they might hoard, or knew people who did. What was clear to me was that I needed to develop the piece.

I was encouraged to apply for the Pleasance and Theatre Royal Plymouth Regional Partnership and the play was selected. With funding from Arts Council England I then developed the piece as a 60-minute monologue, changing the name to *Breathless,* which for me really encompassed the feelings of suffocation and elation.

In the play I wanted to address the sliding scale of hoarding and collecting. I didn't think of myself as a hoarder for a long time because media portrayals were so extreme. I knew I was on a knife-edge though, that I could teeter either way. Translating my experience to the stage has been a fascinating process. I didn't want to visualise hoarding so I worked with Theatre Royal Plymouth and director Stephanie Kempson to present a simple set. We were keen to use sound to elevate the subject matter and Verity Standen's acapella compositions seemed to get inside the human experience, really chiming with the moments of anxiety and joy. Alongside Breathless I'm developing a podcast about hoarding called *Hidden by Things*, where people, not their possessions, are the centre of the conversation.

– Laura Horton

BREATHLESS

Laura Horton

Breathless was first previewed on 20 July 2022 at Theatre Royal Plymouth, premiering at Pleasance Courtyard on 3 August 2022.

Characters

SOPHIE, mid-late 30s

JO, Sophie's girlfriend

DAD

MUM

SISTER

KEVIN, a friend

WAITER

CASHIER

MIME ARTIST

PIP, an agent

TREE SURGEON

NAVAL MAN

JOURNALIST

VAN LADY

LADY

FRIENDS

Notes:

/ is an interruption. An ellipsis (...) can indicate a pause, but also a shift in thought or energy

The play was written as a one-woman show, however it could also be performed by several actors.

1.

Sophie addresses her date, Jo, on her doorstep; it's the end of the evening and another wonderful time together.

SOPHIE That meringue, fuck me.

And the starter - delicious! The sauce was – wow – and that orange wine... I didn't even know orange wine was a thing!

It was well-bodied!

I'm going to be dreaming about that wine for...

Well not just the wine, no!

Thank you for walking me home again, you didn't have to.

You really didn't! I can look after myself, you know. I am a grown-ass...

Oh really? Well, so do you.

That's very presumptuous!

Is that a fact? Is it an, what are we... eight dates... an eight date rule?

What! Six dates? Are you sure? Does the mini-break count as one?

Oh, in a good way. In a very good way!

There is a long lingering moment between them – it could be a kiss or holding each-other's faces, something meaningful.

Come in?

Sophie's tone changes, she's panicked.

Oh... I... Erm...

I thought I said about that early start?

I know, it's just...

It's not that, I mean I'd love you to... and you will, just not...

I still have that mouse, remember? My own danger mouse. It just won't go anywhere, no matter how nicely I ask it. I know you hate mice so...

I know we can't, I appreciate your mum wouldn't love to hear...

No no, it's not that...

I know you would.

Yeah yeah, I know it's temporary.

But that won't be long right?

How long?!

No I don't think you're being too forward.

I just... I just...

There's all the time in the world to see my place.

I think that's a bit unfair.

I wouldn't say snail...

Or sloth, actually.

I'm okay with that, aren't you?

Well then, maybe we could go for a wander? It's dark... a cheeky finger at the shelter on the hill could be fun?!

No?

I'm still...

I'm really into this, into you. You must know that by now?

Please. Don't.

I'm not territorial, I'm really not.

I just, I just...

Don't go. Jo, Jo... JO?

Pause for disappointment.

2.

To audience.

SOPHIE   We have our first date at Positanos, this lovely little family-run Italian. We sit at a table with a tapered candle jammed into an old wine bottle and layered with years of melted wax.

Over the evening, I imagine the exchanges that might've happened over that bottle: reasons for breaking up, for getting together or back together, dirty talk - wanted and unwanted - birthday songs, plotting and planning, dreaming, daydreaming, remembering, celebrating.

I think I read somewhere that liquids retain memory. Is hot wax a liquid? Maybe there are conversations solidified there. Maybe ours will be. I like the idea that an object could preserve something so transient...

Apparently it's an institution, this place. She tells me not to order the bruschetta:

JO   "They'll bring you some for free".

And they do! Two thick slices of grilled bread, piled high with ripe tomatoes, herbs, and drizzled with olive oil.

I mean that's already a great date right there, isn't it?

Great until I start eating it, staining my shirt and getting herbs caught in my teeth.

JO "You've just got a little bit of... nearly, just to the right, still there... still there... little bit to the left... more to the right... got it."

SOPHIE And there's a lot – a lot – of garlic!

JO "But we're both eating it, so..."

SOPHIE It turns out Jo's a freelance chef, working in a little patisserie. She says she likes to try out new recipes on friends and family. Win – if this goes well.

We have loads in common. We don't just share a similar taste in music – I'm embarrassed to remember the days when liking the same bands felt like you were soul mates. We're just on the same wavelength: politically, morally, socially. And we agree on scones, how best to eat them... coming from Devon that's important.

It's one of those ridiculous, rare evenings where the hours feel like minutes. Where the brushing of our forearms feels electric, and every look between us sends blood pumping to – well, you know where.

When Jo goes to the loo, I push my forefinger and thumb into the wax. Hot, uncomfortable, then warm and pliable. When Jo sits back down, she touches the wax too, her fingers, her prints, slightly – ever so slightly – over mine.

The staff are too polite to tell us to piss off so we sit, oblivious, past closing time, sipping our limoncellos and smiling gormlessly at each other – or, at least I am.

It isn't until we hear a polite yawn that we notice the time and glance to see the poor waiter falling off his seat. We leave quickly and apologetically – Jo a normal amount, and me at least twenty times. I think about taking the nub of the extinguished candle at the centre of our table, but decide it's not worth the risk of Jo seeing.

As I close the door I overhear the waiter say:

WAITER   "I just didn't want to hurry love."

SOPHIE   I turn puce.

My body is thumping and fluttering. I try to put my coat on.

The arm holes are ripped and just that bit too small. Jo pretends not to see...

I try to smell my breath on my palm.

I'm terrible at the end of a date. I've often ended dates with a back pat or a handshake – I once told a man he reminded me of my brother. Not because he did, I guess I just panicked.

I race through the excruciating 'what if's' of this moment:

What if we kiss and my breath is so bad she gags?

What if we kiss and bang teeth?

What if we kiss and bang teeth and her tooth falls out?

What if she finds me revolting?

What if I'm the worst kiss she's ever had and I become a story she tells via some viral tweet?

I love kissing, I really do – when it's underway. It's just getting to that point that makes me feel violently sick.

We walk to the end of the road in silence. I have nothing, not even weather-chat.

As we turn the corner she takes my sweaty palm and turns me towards her, I know she's going to kiss me, I'm convinced I still have food stuck in my teeth, I'm worried I might head-butt her, and instead of just letting it happen...

Jo, I need to tell you something.

What am I doing?

JO	"Oh, shit. You're married or something, aren't you?"
SOPHIE	No, no, nothing like that. It's just. This is my... first time.

I don't know why I decide that this is the point to share this particular piece of news.

JO	"Okay...?"
SOPHIE	My first date... with a woman.

She stares at me.

Oh God. I shouldn't have told her this early on, before anything has even happened.

Or actually, have I left it too late? Should I have told her right away? Like, opened with it when we matched? Should I just have it on my profile – I want to date women. I just haven't done it yet?

I can't gauge her response at all – half smirk, half furrowed brow.

(*To Jo*)   Look, I didn't want you to think I was just some straight woman trying things out.

(*To audience*) I shudder. The cold is seeping under my skin. We swirl in this moment... I wait for her verdict.

Pause.

I remember having a chat with my dad when I was 14 or so. We were in the car, waiting for my mum to get out of the hairdressers. Radio Five Live was playing – the crackling of cricket commentary, except, the commentary wasn't actually about cricket.

Something about sandwich fillings. Cream teas.

Our breath was visible. We stared out at the empty carpark – the wall-to-wall graffiti – muddy boots on our feet, winter coats on our backs, our dog on the backseat, contented and wet from a walk. Pens, some with lids, some without, lolled about on the dashboard.

I have no idea why, I went to mum for emotional things, usually, but I just turned to him and said:

I think I like girls, Dad.

We sat in silence for a bit. Then he turned his head, vaguely, in my direction:

DAD	"Sure. Right. Cool. Okay. Sure... okay, cool. Fine. Yeah. Good."
SOPHIE	And then he bought us some fried chicken and turned on Radio 1 for me.

I felt liberated that I'd shared this, then embarrassed, then, for the next twenty-four years I did nothing about it. Painfully shy, I only really went out with people who asked me and they tended to be cocky men – and I do fancy men too – but when I got to thirty-eight, fresh out of another break up... I realised I couldn't ignore this anymore.

I sat with my mum out on the patio last year, halfway through a second bottle of rosé, citronella tealights, and a bowl of Co-Op strong salt and vinegar crisps between us – and I told her I liked women too. Before she could reply, I burst into tears – it was pure relief. She put her hand on mine.

MUM   "Soph, if you want to lick a fanny, lick a fanny."

Pause.

SOPHIE   Jo's still looking at me.

(*To Jo*)   And your profile was so great, and I just, I just... tonight was so...

(*To audience*) She gently tucked my hair behind my ear, grazing my neck and then she kissed me with an intensity that let me know for certain it didn't matter, or at least not right now.

She tasted of coffee, lemon, cream, mint and a hint of garlic.

3.

SOPHIE   I moved into my flat in January. I didn't think for a second that I'd ever live in my very own place, but then again, I never thought I'd leave London.

I went up to London in my mid-twenties for an office job and eventually managed to forge a bit of a writing career – short stories, press releases and the odd article – working in a little coffee shop to supplement my rent.

Like millions of others, the dream was to write a novel. But that could wait.

I loved everything about it – that it was sprawling and historic, full of opportunities and ambition. On any given night you could find anything to do: talks with experts about black holes; verbatim plays about sex work; seminars about grief; subtitled films in parking lots; cocktail parties with views of the river and sample sales where designer clothes were affordable.

I only left because I was evicted.

LANDLORD "That's life, I'm afraid, Sharon."

SOPHIE   It's Sophie.

He was selling one of his thirty properties to pay for his kid's private education. When he picked up the keys, he told me how hard it was being a landlord.

I'd hoped to stay with my housemates, Liz and Michelle, but they had other plans – Liz was to move in with her boyfriend, and

Michelle with other friends. We'd been living there for six years.

I looked around at other house shares, but the thought of moving in with strangers – having to fit all my stuff into a new space – was too much. I just couldn't do it. So I moved home with my parents, to my childhood bedroom in Plymouth, by the sea. My plan was to re-group, save up and move back. I would definitely move back to London.

Liz and Shell moved out a week earlier than me, which upset me, but I didn't say. I thought we'd enjoy those last moments together. I helped them load their vans and offered to help unpack but they both said they'd be fine.

That last week was a haze of fried food, white wine, sobbing, black bags, and boxes. I'd vowed to get rid of some clothes – hauls for charity and for Vinted. I'd make some money in the process. But I only managed to bin one woollen jumper in the end, and that was only because it had moth-holes in the chest. Even that decision took half a day.

And that's it, that's all I chucked.

Moving was change enough.

4.

SOPHIE I've loved clothes for as long as I can remember. When I was three, my mum used to work as a library assistant on a Sunday. It was the one day a week my dad had to dress me, and quite frankly – as much as I loved him – his taste was horrific.

It was a traumatic time.

He'd often forget important things too, like knickers.

On one occasion when he took me in to see my mum for lunch, I was wailing so much she had to intervene. From then on, we'd pick outfits out together and lay them out for my dad the night before. My favourite was the pink corduroy dress and matching jacket my nan had found in a charity shop.

Charity shopping was my thing. The anticipation about what might be there, the digging and trawling and rooting through potential treasures with my mum and nan. Until I was in my mid-twenties, my wardrobe was almost entirely made up of charity shop purchases and January-sale items. I lived for a bargain.

The first memorable designer piece I remember buying was in a tiny vintage shop in Cardiff – until that point, designer for me meant Jaeger. But here was a metallic silver, black and gold Christian Dior pencil skirt with deep, deep pockets. It was £27, which for me at the time was a lot, but it was Dior, and I had never owned such a special item. I hung it above my bed and dreamed of being able to wear it; of being slim enough, so that the waistband wouldn't – just about – do up around my right thigh.

5.

SOPHIE	On the second date with Jo, we played crazy golf.
	I am competitive, a Monica-from-Friends-level-of-competitive, so I was reluctant to take the invitation. But, it turns out my aggressive swinging and grunting really turns her on.
	I mean, Jo still wins, despite my spectacular hole-in-one straight into the mouth of a dinosaur. I congratulate her – even though I call her all-the-cunts-going in my head. I hate losing but I try to do it with grace.
	It turns out Jo is staying with her parents – a move back after a break-up to nurse her wounds and re-group.
JO	"My ex met someone else... she told me, before she started anything. We were in a rut, you know, it took that for me to see. I'm fine with it, we're still friends."
SOPHIE	I am in awe of this because I don't keep in touch with any of my exes – I've never really wanted to.
	I tell Jo about my ex, Pete, who slept with my friend, Angie. When I tried to speak to Ange she told me:
ANGIE	"He didn't come so I didn't count it."
SOPHIE	I didn't realise that was a rule.
	Jo and I talk about our first date.
JO	"I just couldn't tell if you liked me."
SOPHIE	I explain to her what a terrible dater I am. Most people have bad dating stories about

other people; I mainly have bad dating stories about myself.

I regale her with them, even the worst story, the one where I went on a date with opera singer, Ryan, and was so nervous that when I went to the loo and a random lad offered me a line of coke, I happily said yes, thinking it would chill me out, even though I had never taken it before. What I didn't realise was that a) Ryan's friend Lucy had wandered into the toilet and seen me bent over doing drugs with a man who wasn't Ryan, and b) God knows what it was, but it wasn't cocaine. I spent the evening pacing the brown sticky carpet and going:

"I can't sit down, I can't sit down, I can't sit down, I can't sit down – don't make me sit down."

Jo laughs at this, holding my face and kissing my forehead.

JO   "That wouldn't have put me off you, Soph."

SOPHIE   I was the first person Jo matched with. I tell her there's probably much better out there, she gurns at me in response.

She tells me about her plans to travel, how she's given most of her things away, that she could fit the entire contents of her wardrobe into a backpack. I don't believe her.

She says it makes her feel lighter to be free of things; she doesn't like mess and clutter. Her ex had taken up most of the shared wardrobe and she'd struggled with the hurricane of things left around the house.

JO "She had over thirty pairs of shoes! Insane!"

Pause for Sophie to take this comment in.

SOPHIE We're near mine tonight.

JO "Which flat is yours?"

SOPHIE I point at it and she lingers. We have a peck.

JO "I can walk you home?"

SOPHIE I smile. I tell her it's fine. I scuttle off.

6.

SOPHIE When I was leaving London, I rented a woman with a van to drive the five hours back to my parents. She was un-phased by my piles of stuff.

VAN LADY "I've seen it all, love."

SOPHIE She was a genius at tessellation, and when we shut the van, every inch of space was accounted for.

My parents hadn't hesitated about welcoming me home, but when I pulled up with that van, that enormous vehicle, they went white.

DAD "I thought you didn't have any furniture?"

SOPHIE I don't, Dad.

We unpacked in silence, and by the time we were finished my bedroom was stacked. There was a tiny walkway to the bed, and bags and boxes in the hallway, bathroom, living room and kitchen.

There were tears.

I promised and vowed to clear things away. I would sort myself out and move back to London as soon as I could, much lighter than when I arrived.

7.

SOPHIE   When I was twenty-four, I was shortlisted for the Vogue Talent competition for emerging writers. I could never afford the magazine, but saw the opportunity in a copy left behind on the bus.

One of the three pieces I had to write was a short autobiography. I found it typed up under my bed when I moved back in.

Sophie gets a piece of paper out of her pocket and reads some of it aloud.

Aged seven, I got over-excited by talk of a club that my school friends were going to – the Brownies. I had some kind of idea that, maybe, this club was somewhere you went to eat biscuits, baked goods, of the same name. On finding out that there was a uniform and it was – of all things – yellow and brown, I was mortified. Clearly the world was a scary place.

Had the Brownies been the Barbara Cartland Pinkies, worn wings, leg warmers and spandex tights, I would have signed up like a shot. But I avoided that type of dysfunctional socialising. I never won a badge for tea-making or tent-erecting. The only pink things I ever came across were medicines for threadworm, a flasher in the park, and blancmange.

'My pink stage' came to an abrupt end, though, aged 10 when I discovered Blur, a pair of Levi 501's, and Doc Martin boots. Out went the fluffy outfits and the hot pink pants. The pink little ponies, once the object of my desire, were made bald, courtesy of the kitchen scissors. This was liberation indeed.

She puts the piece of paper away.

There was a lunch for the shortlisted candidates. I went up to London on the megabus. I didn't know what to expect. What to say? What to wear – what the fuck do you wear to Vogue? My spanx cut into my belly and I tottered awkwardly in my heels. On arrival, I met the shortlist in the flesh, half of which already seemed to know people in the office, waving at Tilly by the window, and asking after Lucy's father, arranging to go to the Groucho for drinks. I had no idea what, or where, the Groucho was at the time – I imagined a little grotto.

I sat quietly throughout the afternoon, carefully considering my words, how I ate, lifted my cutlery, and crossed my legs.

I couldn't maintain eye contact with anyone, didn't manage anything witty or charming. The others listed off designers and fashion photographers, name-dropped influential people they knew, talked about the colleges they went to.

When asked where I went to school, one lady looked quizzical at the name of my comprehensive.

I couldn't keep up. Though I wanted that opportunity more than anything, instinctively I knew I was not right for it. I didn't have the right clothes, the poise, or...

Pause.

And then I got it and I was sure there had been some kind of mistake.

I could barely afford to be in London – I stayed on a friend's sofa. I got the bus to work. A ninety-minute commute. I couldn't afford to go with colleagues for lunches, and I'm sure I was laughed at when I pulled out my foil-wrapped sandwiches. I ended up eating in the toilets or in shop changing rooms. I made myself ill with anxiety and couldn't make it in that final week because a stomach upset kept me pinned to the toilet.

I didn't realise it was a big deal at the time – had no idea how to leverage it – and when it ended, and I came home, it just felt like a failure. The whole experience.

I knew then that I wanted to move to London, though; I wanted to become more stylish. I wanted clothes I couldn't afford. I wanted to be better.

8.

SOPHIE Because of Jo's job, it's hard to see much of her, but we text and send voicenotes every day. We speak on the phone before bed; she even sends me postbox flowers. It's sickening and absolutely fantastic.

We plan our third date, a boat trip and a walk around a country park. It's a grey day, but when the sun comes out, it casts swords of light on the boat as it cuts through the water.

Jo ruffles my hair and puts her arms around me.

I used to work in the Orangery here when I was a teenager.

(To Jo) See that bench, I always wanted to have sex there.

JO "You still can."

Sophie looks to the audience as if to say 'and we did' but she gives no detail away.

SOPHIE We buy hot chocolate and wander the grounds. When we look at each other, I get this feeling – one they only tell you about in films and romantic poems.

That is, until it gets to the very end of the day. I dance around having to get home, having to leave.

9.

SOPHIE   When I moved back in with my family, far from bucking up and sorting myself out, I regressed. It was like I was a child again, bickering with my little sister.

SISTER   "Oh my god, it'll never suit you, just let me have it."

SOPHIE   Having my meals cooked for me, needing my mum for hugs and my dad for lifts into town.

I found things in my room long forgotten, under beds and behind bookcases: a chalkboard with "Go For It!" etched in my mum's handwriting. She'd written it when I was ill and grieving my Nan during GCSEs. I found angsty diaries with entries that made my toes curl – Hayden Peter looked at me for ten seconds today; I think he must love me.

I unearthed Teddy Polar – my favourite cuddly toy, the one I would cling to in my pram and wail when dropped. I found ripped band posters and old tie-dye vests, baggy jeans with beer stains and friendship bracelets.

It also threw up invisible things, those that had been dormant in my brain: my dad carrying me up the stairs to bed, the day he told me sadly he couldn't do it anymore, I was too old, it was hurting his back.

DAD   "You were sixteen, Sophie."

SOPHIE   I was actually nine.

The shock of my period and getting sticky sanitary wings caught on my bits, not knowing how to cope with the cramps. Growing underarm hair in primary school, feeling shame when the boys in gym class started laughing and pointing at it.

Finding my Mum's contraception cap and putting it on my head. Wrestling matches with my sister and heart-shaped bruises. Trying and failing to make edible food. Throwing up over the neighbour's wall and getting the key stuck in the door at 3am.

Paralytic kisses at house parties and stair-slumped-sobbing after nights out, drunk and rejected.

An anxious brain I didn't understand.

But I'm not one of those women from the Channel 5 Christmas films, coming home from the big city, successful and victorious to find love with my school sweetheart, or an award-winning filmmaker reconnecting with my hometown. I plod back to my parent's house with nothing much to show for my city life, save a pickled liver, a head-butted heart, rejection letters, and many things.

10.

SOPHIE In my second week in London, walking home with a bag of discounted food, I noticed a glittery sign with an arrow – Sample Sale Ten Metres. I followed the arrow to a glass-boxed space with fairy lights and rows and rows and rows of clothes, in every shape, colour and style imaginable.

I stepped inside and a glass of prosecco was thrust into my hand – free fizz? Oh my God, geddon! A diffuser chuffed out tangerine scents, jazz music wafted out of a small speaker. It was quiet, too – barely anyone in there.

I began eyeing up the aisles, doing a few laps before I tucked in. I picked up a long blue lace dress with a cape. It was love at first sight. I was starving for this dress. I looked at the label, £475. Okay, fuck no. I decided to try and get away with one more glass of prosecco and leave.

Just before I did though, I spotted a poster on the wall, a wall chart with coloured dots and prices. Yellow – £60, blue – £40, pink – £20, white – £10. I looked at the label on this lace dress – pink. This dress was £20!

I could not believe how much money I would be saving if I bought this dress.

Then I saw a cream tulle skirt twinkling. Glitter boobs, willies, and fannies embellished it. I threw it over my arm. I saw a floor-length coat with an appliqué red bow and arrow, and a pair of high-waisted electric blue skater trousers. Then I spied another amazing thing, and then another, and another, and another, and I knew exactly where I'd wear each item, and exactly how I'd feel when I did.

I left that first sale with five bags of clothes, heart full and tingling. That night I danced around my little bedroom, unable to believe my luck.

I was on my way.

Pause.

After a while, my room in London became a carefully constructed maze.

Spare bits of floor became storage solutions, my desk was stacked to the ceiling with books, hundreds of nails, tapped badly into the walls, held hangers, which held more and more clothes. It was a smallish room with a Victorian fireplace and two double wardrobes, both stuffed to the brim.

I rarely invited anyone in – and by rarely, I mean never.

My housemates never poked their heads in. I'd always go to friend's places, stay over at boyfriends. My bedroom was a space for me. A room packed with trinkets – treasures that charted my life from newborn to now. I didn't want anyone intruding on that.

And then one day when I was lying on my bed watching videos of mini things made out of felt, the door opened.

KEVIN   "Fucking hell, Soph."

SOPHIE   I jumped and toppled off the pile of clothes I'd been balancing on.

KEVIN   "I was knocking but you didn't hear."

SOPHIE   My friend Kevin stood in the doorframe.

KEVIN   "If that fell on you, you could die."

SOPHIE   He gesticulated to a floor-to-ceiling shoe holder which teetered dangerously under the weight of double the shoes it was advertised to hold.

He picked up a daisy-hemmed purple cotton dress that wouldn't pull down past my tits. I'd drunkenly tried it on last week and nearly got stuck.

A dress I vowed to wear one day, like so many things in this room. Like pretty much everything in this room.

He said he'd come over to drop off a book he'd borrowed, but had really come to moan about a bad date. We never ended up talking about his love life, though. Instead, the shock on his face prompted something deep and unwelcome in the pit of my belly.

11.

SOPHIE   I said I'd stay with my parents for a month, but that turned into just over a year. I found better ways to store my clothes so it wasn't quite so intrusive for them. I had numerous afternoons with my mum where she tried to help me throw things away but they just ended in arguments. When it came to my clothes I was a lioness – they were my pride.

I lost touch with a lot of London friends. I barely heard from my old housemates. I went underground. I kept an eye on house shares but couldn't afford anything and after a while realised I couldn't move back, not with the best will in the world.

It felt like I was hurtling towards forty with no direction. Not spending money on travel, rent, clothes, eating out, though, I managed to save much more than I'd anticipated. I picked up some marketing shifts and kept myself busy with work. My parents urged me to look for my own place. It took four months to find my flat and seven stressful months to buy it. A little one-bed off a cobbled lane with scalloped-edged walls and low ceilings.

I'm not used to living alone and not having much to do of an evening – London had too much choice, this too little. So, I started dating.

The first was a curly-haired tree surgeon with huge hands, totally different to the men I'd dated before. Naturally, I thought it might actually work. Roll on four months, and he turned out to be another gaslighter with a drink problem, no interest in making me cum, and little-to-no capacity for kindness.

The last thing he shouted at me was:

TREE SURGEON "I don't want to end up in one of your stories, Sophie..."

SOPHIE   Well, what can you do?

The next was an estate-agent-turned-avant-garde-mime-artist – his words not mine, who made his own socks. We had two weeks of giddy fucking; it was great until he turned out to be addicted to sexting other women.

MIME ARTIST "If you like me, it's something you'll have to accept."

SOPHIE   The next, an angry Naval man, who talked about himself persistently, and proceeded to send furious messages when I wouldn't send naked photos.

NAVAL MAN "You must have body issues love."

SOPHIE   None of them came to the flat. They liked to be in range of their own things, X-Boxes, cock rings, bulk powder – there was no curiosity in coming here, which was much better for me. How I wanted it.

When I moved into my flat, I really intended to chuck things away. Clear out, not bring everything I owned into this new space. It was going to be an entirely fresh start. I moved my stuff over slowly at first, little by little so as not to overwhelm myself, keeping it out of the way of my parents.

I knew I had too much stuff, but the idea of moving through the world without these things, with no armoury to head back to at the end of the day, just wasn't a world I wanted to live in. I also knew it wasn't a world I could sustain living in for much longer.

My sister tried to help me move some things over... but her unhelpful comments included:

SISTER   "Oh my god – this wouldn't have fit you when you were six."

SISTER   "You really should think about the environment more, like I do."

SISTER   "What happens to your stuff when you die?"

It's this comment that stops me in my tracks. The thought of leaving my things in the world without me, not knowing where or who they'll end up with, makes me short of breath.

12.

SOPHIE   On our fourth date, Jo invites me to her auntie's cottage for five whole days.

We drive up to South Wales in her Ford Focus and pitch up with bags of wine and food from Lidl, cheap champagne, pizza and hundreds of packets of crisps.

We light the fire and we nest.

It's easy. I mean, fuck me, she actually thinks about things I might like. If I have a problem, she'll talk to me about it. I never knew it could be like this.

We crunch the leaves on our walks through the forest and she tells me about her family, her break-ups, her dad dying. She tells me about a health scare she had.

We speak like old friends and new lovers. We hold hands and clutch waists and kiss softly.

She asks about the flat a lot, she can't wait to have her own space. She wants to know how I've decorated it, how large it is, what bed sheets I use, how big the windows are, what the light is like in the living room.

I manage to side-step most questions.

She's very keen to come over.

Sophie looks panicked.

13.

SOPHIE   Kevin is a journalist and just after I get back from my mini-break with Jo, he phones me.

KEVIN   "Soph', do you want to do an interview for a broadsheet newspaper?"

SOPHIE   I was fucking ecstatic. Yes! I'm finally getting somewhere, writer Sophie Carter...

KEVIN   "It's about hoarding being re-classified as a mental health disorder."

SOPHIE	What?
	He goes quiet, like he realises where he might've gone wrong in this conversation.
KEVIN	"My editor wants me to write a piece by tomorrow and I just thought..."
SOPHIE	I'm not a hoarder, Kev.
KEVIN	"You have a lot of stuff..."

Pause.

KEVIN	"It's just we've had a few conversations about it now... normally involving pints of wine sure, but..."

SOPHIE (*To audience*) I think I blocked that out.

I think I blocked a lot of things out. Like the fact my housemates did actually end up living together – I found out on Instagram, a photo in their immaculate new flat. When I asked, they pretended it was just circumstance, things falling through. I knew, though. I couldn't have been easy to live with.

KEVIN	"They want a younger voice for the piece, they don't just want to represent the hoarder SOS stereotype."
SOPHIE	I've started crying and I'm desperate for him not to hear.
KEVIN	"I know you're not rats, paintpots filled with shit, newspapers-to-the-ceiling bad, and I'm not saying you ever will be, but doesn't it all start somewhere? Have you even let anyone over yet?"
SOPHIE	No, but I haven't had time to decorate.

KEVIN   "It'll only end up being a line or two, in
            a much wider piece – we can make you
            anonymous if you like... I won't push you, I
            just thought it might help."

SOPHIE   I'll think about it.

            I hang up and turn my phone off.

                         14.

SOPHIE   The fifth date – although it feels like we'd
            been dating forever, is to see a play – a new
            one-person show in the local theatre about
            a woman's journey to an OCD diagnosis.

            I thought OCD was mainly hand washing
            and ritual, but she talks a lot about control,
            the obsessive nature of her thoughts and
            the way she sometimes imagines the most
            horrific things – like her nan licking her
            out, or a dog mauling a baby.

            Not things she wants – just things that
            creep in when she's anxious, things that are
            impossible to explain without looking like a
            pervert.

            After the show the plan is to go for tapas
            and wine in the restaurant opposite.

            I've been coming to this place since I was
            a teenager. One tapas is a full meal. There
            are high stools, paintings of matadors and
            aubergines.

            I thought we'd have loads to talk about
            over our albondigas and patatas bravas,
            we usually did, but conversation is quiet
            and muted. Not on her part – she's always

engaging – but bits of the play stick in my head. Jo asks if I'm okay. I tell her it's work, which is partly true.

Jo's mum is away so she invites me to stay. She says her room hasn't changed much since she was a teenager, though she didn't care if it did. She's not the nostalgic sort. Not like me.

There are a few Buffy posters, a framed photograph of Blondie, a lumpy bed, some comic books, a lava lamp, one neat box of schoolwork, one cuddly toy and one old school tie. A tiny clothes rail with one pair of jeans, a few t-shirts, two jumpers, one dress and one, two, three pairs of shoes. The entirety of her possessions.

Fuck me.

15.

Sophie addresses this next part to many different people.

SOPHIE Oh, my place? no that won't work, I've just moved in, see, don't have a bed just yet.

Bed bugs. I'm sleeping on the sofa at the moment, so still not the best set-up for le sex.

My mum's coming tomorrow and I've just washed the sheets.

Your place is much nicer.

I've got a ladybug infestation.

Yours is much closer.

The toilet's blocked and you'll probably need the loo at some point, right?

There's a snake on the loose in the area apparently, can we go to yours?

I can't lock the door, and someone might break in.

My sister's staying and she's a twat.

I think I might have an angry ghost.

These are just some of the excuses I've used to not have people over and some of them I used on Jo.

My flat isn't something you'd recognise from hoarding programmes on TV but if you walked in, you'd know there was an issue.

I really wanted to make sure it didn't become this.

But as I brought things over I found reasons, deep motivations, to keep it all. As I opened suction pack after suction pack, the clothes, they breathed heavy sighs of relief.

My parents met me at the flat the day I got the keys, brought Cava. It was empty and light and full of possibility then.

They came over once again early on when I'd only just furnished it from marketplace, and had only pulled over a few boxes from storage, but never since. I always visit them and get irritable when they push to come here.

You can't see the bedroom floor for clothes. It's not easy to open the door. The rails on the wardrobe are always breaking under the weight. You can't move simply between things. My flat is stuffed with possessions and the recollections I attach to them. I feel equally suffocated and sated by my things.

Pause.

SOPHIE *(To Jo)* I'm not territorial about my space, I'm really not.

JO   "You are. I can't keep doing this jig with you."

SOPHIE *(To Jo)* I just, I just...

JO   "You just –?"

Pause.

SOPHIE   Don't go. Jo, Jo... JO?

Later that night she sent me a voicenote:

JO   "I can't do this anymore. Something's going on, stop pretending, Sophie."

SOPHIE   I try to phone her, but she ignores all my calls. Then I construct a very long voicenote which I delete and just text:

I was never pretending, Jo – I'm so sorry if that's what it felt like, please don't do this. Please?

I text again, and again a few days later, and again a few days after that.

Jo, I'm so sorry, it's really not what you think.

She doesn't respond.

I feel manic; I never thought we wouldn't speak. I thought she was going to be a long-term fixture.

I go charity shopping, I scour TK Maxx many times, and I rummage through clearance sections adding to my piles of things.

16.

SOPHIE   After I did the interview I told Kevin I was happy for him to use my name. Fuck it! What's the worst that could happen? He told me I could always change my mind, I had a bit of time.

This is recorded from the interview with Kevin.

SOPHIE V/O I knew there was an issue, kind of. I'd hide bags when I came in the door because my housemates would get agitated. I'd lie about how much I was buying. I put sales ahead of everything. Remember when I said I couldn't make your birthday? Both times. I'm so sorry, Kev. It just mounted up, I couldn't chuck anything away. Mum said I've always been like that. I just kept buying.

No no no, I never got in debt, the clothes were mostly cheaper than the high street. I've just spent on the wrong things, haven't I, Kev?

I don't know why I did it... does it have to be one thing? I never felt comfortable in myself. I couldn't process things maybe, like grief and break-ups, I don't know, I just couldn't. And maybe creating little fantasy worlds, well it felt manageable. Does that make sense? When you struggle with yourself, making up better versions is comforting – it just makes me feel safe.

She starts crying on the recording. Sophie on-stage is struggling to know how to react.

SOPHIE   We talked about what I intended to do. I found this bit harder as I hadn't intended to do anything.

He told me he'd let me know when it was out and I forgot about it – I was loved up, I was giddy and then I was heartbroken.

Then I woke up late on a Friday morning to thirty-six missed calls from my mum, Dad and Kevin and a number of texts from friends.

FRIEND1:   "You're so brave, lovely."

FRIEND2:   "You okay?"

FRIEND3:   "I can't believe you didn't say anything, babe."

FRIEND4:   "I should've noticed, I'm a bad friend."

SOPHIE   I listen to the first voicemail from my mum.

MUM   "Have you seen the paper, flowerpot?"

SOPHIE   My stomach lurches, but I can't tell yet if this is a good or a bad thing. I pull my jacket over my pyjamas, wrap it around me and run to the corner shop.

I spot the paper – a national paper.

My face beaming out of the front page, a recent photo from my Facebook. There is a mass of hoarding, books, boxes and things that aren't mine, superimposed behind my head and the title:

'My Life as a Hoarder'.

I buy all the copies in the shop and shake and wobble as I pace home.

Kevin sounds panicked on the phone.

KEVIN   "I'm so sorry, that was the subs – I had no idea they would do that."

SOPHIE   I'm glad he doesn't live nearby anymore. I know he'd be on my doorstep and I just need to be alone. I don't know how I feel – it's a mixture of sickness and adrenalin. The photo has a small stain over my forehead, making it look like I haven't washed. I don't love that fucking picture either.

I spend four days at home. My brain is too anxious to let me just lie in bed, so I pace the flat a lot and scroll through my phone. I use up the last of the cupboard food: pesto, pasta, Monster Munch. I have to leave the house eventually for coffee, I can't live without it.

The article is actually lovely. Really well rounded, informative, kind, and I get lots of comments from strangers online, nice ones.

Lots of people have problems with things it would seem.

Three weeks go by and I'm fine – despite the occasional wobble when I think how many people have seen the piece.

I've had to acknowledge that maybe there are changes to be made. But slowly, very slowly.

I get phone calls from tabloids.

TABLOID JOURNO "We'll offer you 600 quid for an article about your hoarding."

SOPHIE But they wanted to make it seem as extreme as possible.

TABLOID JOURNO "Let's pile up all your clothes and we can photograph you with your head sticking out of the top?"

SOPHIE I say no, despite how helpful the money would be.

A production company want me to take part in a documentary where they pair you up with another 'collector' and you clear out each other's things.

(*To producer*) But I'd have a breakdown on air.

He nods as if to say: Exactly.

I turn it all down apart from a first-person article in a women's magazine where they encourage me to write about my experience of hoarding in my own voice. It's unpaid but I want to find words for this.

I am a fucking writer after all.

17.

SOPHIE I decide to go to London for a few days. I want a distraction, I miss the pace of it; I find a cheap hotel with a shared bathroom. I get the train so I can work without feeling sick. The plan is to get this piece written and edited while I'm here; the deadline coincides with my train back.

On the way up, I text Liz and Michelle and try not to look at Jo's social media. My heart both springs and drops as I spot a sale I'd love to go to and two more that are surely worth a punt. A designer I love – 90% off. I start to plan my route to the shop. Figure out how much money I can spend, think about the clothes I might find. How glorious it will be to be back in the city, swinging bags of important clothes back to my hotel room.

I eat my lunch by 11am, a Boots meal deal, and by the time I arrive at 1pm I'm bored and hungry again. I haven't managed to write anything.

I've arranged dinner instead with my old friend Caroline. We normally see each other every few years, mostly keeping up with each other online. Caz has an enviable life, a beautiful partner, a wonderful job, an airy, light flat. She talks about herself endlessly but she's also very funny and that is absolutely what I need – not to discuss myself. I walk and I walk, one hour and forty-five minutes to my destination. I drop my bags and check my phone, nothing from Liz or Michelle. I wonder if I should text anyone else while I'm here. There are lots of people to see but I don't think I've got the energy.

As I get ready to head out, I instinctively scroll through social media, cave, and look at Jo's profile. She's not posted anything for weeks. At first, I find it comforted me, but now I worry it's because she's too busy having a great time. I flick my thumb until it hurts – I imagine that the social media generations will all have arthritic thumbs. Liz has posted a photo, Michelle standing behind her with a drink and another woman I don't know. I like it so they remember I exist.

I look through Jo's likes on Twitter but nothing interesting comes up. Then, I see a tweet; a book agent is inviting people to a walk at Hilly Fields tomorrow, a chance for writers to connect and to pitch. I'd love to go to this but it clashes with the sale. I wouldn't have the guts to pitch anyway... I'd just be awkward and leave, annoyed at myself.

Just as I'm about to leave the hotel I get a text from Caroline, cancelling. She's got a work dinner she forgot about, apparently. I grab some sushi and I hole up in my hotel room. I have a bath, watch Poirot, and I set my alarm early.

18.

SOPHIE   I want to be the first at this sale and I schlep off across London – three tubes and a bus, forgoing my complimentary continental breakfast. My deadline is tomorrow so I'll head to a café afterwards to write and then try and make it to a gallery, maybe a walk around the Thames.

It's quite quiet at the sale - I'm struck by the beauty of freelancing, the weekday freedom. I spot things I love and gather them up hungrily – it's been a while since I was in this environment and it feels safe, familiar, and dangerously exciting.

My feet pinch, I've worn silly shoes – leather trainers with 'oui' and 'non' on the right and left toes, and they're not worn-in yet. A lot of the shoes I own are lovely but very uncomfortable. I don't try anything on, I never do, I avoid that humiliation. My arms ache under the bulk of pastel dresses, beaded skirts, furry neon coats and embellished shirts as I queue to pay.

I lay everything on the desk, eleven beautiful items.

CASHIER   "Lovely haul you have here! Good eye."

The cashier tots everything up.

I start to cry.

She stares at me.

I apologise for my outburst and I take my card out.

19.

SOPHIE   I couldn't tell you how many sales I've been to over the years, except to say it would be in the hundreds.

Some were a lot more expensive, some cheaper. Established, mid-range, and new designers. At some there were fights, or queues wrapping around the block. Some were empty and you could haggle. I once pulled a sickie and travelled to zone six to a sale where everything was a tenner: silk jumpsuits, wool coats, leather skirts, and embroidered jackets.

I went to another the day after major surgery and nearly collapsed on a pensioner.

Another, where I followed a woman around for two hours while she decided if she wanted this beautiful floral ball gown – she put it down and hallelujah, it was mine! Another ball gown I would never wear. I think I have five now.

There were versions of me in all of those clothes. The confident artiste, the sexual adventurer, the Booker-winning author, Earth Mother, funny daughter, quirky lover, renowned journalist, the best date, and I would keep buying and keep buying to find more and more...

Pause.

The night before my train to London, I'd been packing. I wanted a backpack so I could easily walk around without dragging a case. I poured myself a glass of wine, and started to appraise the rest of my wardrobe, as I often did.

Bubblegum pink, the skirt version of the Killing Eve dress, a skull suit worn by Skin from Skunk Anansie and a Cambridge Rucksack donated by Annie Lennox – all bought cheaply at a charity sale in East London. A yellow large-knit jumper with balloon sleeves, a silk dress screen printed with the French Riviera – sea, stripes, red lipstick, fishing boats, champagne. I have beautiful things. It's a shame they don't fit.

I plonked myself on the floor and spilled my wine. It felt like a wave of hate was coming from all these unworn, hidden outfits. These potential people. These ghosts.

20.

SOPHIE I make it to the park, sweaty and flustered. I am forty-five minutes late. I see a group of about thirty people meandering up the hill. I hesitate, I can't just join them.

I try to hold my shopping bags discreetly, but they're heavy and weighing me down.

I walk up to the group and a woman welcomes me in, another writer. There is a swell of people around the agent and I know I won't be able to speak to her, but I talk to four other people about their pitches and ideas and it's lovely to have creative conversations.

Everyone goes for coffee and the agent, Pip, stands and thanks everyone for coming.

PIP "The only person who hasn't pitched is you."

SOPHIE She points at me. One lady looks sadly at me as if I've really messed up.

PIP "I'm going to come and have a coffee with you."

SOPHIE Then, the woman glares at me. Pip sits next to me and I am filled with gratitude. Who says you have to crawl up someone's backside in order to be heard?

PIP "What is it you want to write about?"

SOPHIE I hesitate, I stumble a little, then I tell her I want to write about hoarding. I tell her a little bit about my story, pushing my bags under the stool. She nods.

PIP "When you've written it, send it straight to me."

SOPHIE She passes me her card and she leaves.

After that, I get on the tube and head back to the sale.

(To cashier) I'm so sorry, but can I return these?

The cashier points to a no returns policy.

A lady in the sale asks what I bought, I show her.

LADY "I'll buy them off you."

21.

SOPHIE   I phone my mum on the train back to my hotel, buzzing. I am lighter than I've been for years. I find my article flows quickly that evening. I write smoothly and edit on the way home, getting the piece in just on time.

When it comes out a week later, I spend most of the day with happy tears in my eyes. Lots of people get in touch to tell me it resonated with them, made them feel less alone. I'm contacted by a hoarding charity and by the BBC and Channel 4.

I start to sell things online... just a few things, but it's a start. Now that I'm not in London I don't have the temptation of sample sales, but I avoid clothes shopping and focus on writing and dinners out with friends. I join a wild swimming group and go out for long walks.

I start painting the flat and suction packing things up, just for now, just so it doesn't feel so manic. I buy little candles and much-needed new bed sheets. Ones that make me feel cosy and warm.

A week after the piece comes out, I get a knock at the door. I normally ignore the door, but today, something compels me not to.

(To Jo)   Oh. Hi.

It's Jo. She's staring at me with a look I know well by now.

Pause.

(*To Jo*)   Well, I mean, I didn't know how to...

It was never like that.

You did?

I'm glad you liked it; it took a long time to know how to say it.

Thank you, that means a lot.

Yeah, that was why...

You want to come in?

Erm...

Pause. She's terrified but she knows this moment is pivotal.

JO   Okay.

SOPHIE   Come in...

Sophie leans to one side to allow Jo in and turns to follow her inside.

Lights down.

The end.

More plays by women:

Humane by Polly Creed
ISBN 978-1-912430-57-4 £9.99
Wollstonecraft Live! by Kaethe Fine
ISBN 978-1-912430-61-1 £11.99
Diary of a Hounslow Girl by Ambreen Razia
ISBN 978-0-9536757-9-1 £8.99
Harvest by Manjula Padmanabhan
ISBN 978-0-9536757-7-7 £9.99
Mistaken: Annie Besant in India by Rukhsana
Ahmad ISBN 978-0-9551566-9-4 £7.99
Penetration by Carolyn Lloyd-Davies
ISBN 978-1-912430-63-5 £9.99
The Curious Lives of Shakespeare and Cervantes by Asa
Palomera ISBN 978-1-911501-13-8 £9.99
The Marvellous Adventures of Mary Seacole by Cleo
Sylvestre ISBN 978-1-912430-59-8 £8.99
Three Mothers by Matilda Velevitch
ISBN 978-1-912430-35-2 £9.99

For collections of plays by women:

www.aurorametro.com

Ingram Content Group UK Ltd.
Milton Keynes UK
UKHW020030120723
424867UK00011B/83

9 781912 430833